THAT'S MY JAM!

ELECTRONIC MUSIC

BY HEATHER E. SCHWARTZ

EUREKA!, AN IMPRINT OF BELLWETHER MEDIA BY FLUTTERBEE

eureka!

Eureka! books turn real stories into unforgettable experiences. Clear, direct language and sharp, captivating imagery make it easy to follow your curiosity, one fascinating fact at a time.
Your Eureka! moment awaits!

This edition first published in 2027 by Bellwether Media, Inc.

For information regarding permission, write to Bellwether Media, Inc., Attention: Permissions Department, 3500 American Blvd W, Suite 150, Bloomington, MN 55431.

Library of Congress Cataloging-in-Publication Data

Names: Schwartz, Heather E. author
Title: Electronic music / by Heather E. Schwartz.
Description: Eureka. | Minneapolis : Bellwether Media, Inc, 2027. | Series: That's my jam! | Includes index. | Audience: Ages 9-13 | Audience: Grades 7-9 | Summary: ""Engaging images accompany information on electronic music. The text level and subject matter are intended for students in grades 5 through 9"-Provided by publisher"-- Provided by publisher.
Identifiers: LCCN 2026018761 (print) | LCCN 2026018762 (ebook) | ISBN 9798898801243 (library binding) | ISBN 9798898802486 (ebook)
Subjects: LCSH: Electronic music--History and criticism | Electronica (Music)--History and criticism | Electronic musical instruments--History
Classification: LCC ML1092 .S39 2027 (print) | LCC ML1092 (ebook) | DDC 786.7--dc23/eng/20260414

LC record available at https://lccn.loc.gov/2026018761
LC ebook record available at https://lccn.loc.gov/2026018762

Editor: Ashley Kuehl Designer: Josh Brink

Printed in the United States of America, North Mankato, MN.

TABLE OF CONTENTS

WHAT IS ELECTRONIC?

Electronic music often has wandering melodies. It has mysterious sounds. It may have repetitive rhythms. But what sets this style apart is the way it is made.

STACEY "HOTWAXX" HALE

BJÖRK

CALVIN HARRIS

DAVID GUETTA

Other genres use instruments such as guitar, bass, and drums. Electronic music uses electronic instruments. These can be synthesizers, or synths. They can be drum machines or digital samplers. Electronic music composers create songs. These songs are unlike anything made before. Big artists include Björk and Stacey "Hotwaxx" Hale. David Guetta and Calvin Harris top streaming charts.

THE HISTORY OF ELECTRONIC

Electronic music did not develop in just one place. Artists from around the world influenced one another. They created new sounds over decades.

CLARA ROCKMORE

Many female artists had a hand in early electronic music. Russian artist Clara Rockmore was a famous theremin player. She played in the United States in the 1930s and 1940s. British composer Daphne Oram spliced tape recordings in the 1950s. English artist Delia Derbyshire worked in the 1960s and 1970s. She altered recordings of instruments and natural sounds. She composed the theme for the TV show *Doctor Who.*

The 1970s and 1980s brought new sounds. Many Black and LGBTQ+ DJs combined disco and funk. Chicago DJ Frankie Knuckles created house music. Michigan artists Juan Atkins, Derrick May, and Kevin Saunderson were the Belleville Three. They helped start techno music. In Germany, Kraftwerk made music with synths, drum machines, and vocoders.

EDM

EDM stands for electronic dance music. It includes many subgenres, including house, synthpop, and trance.

Techno took off in Berlin clubs in the 1990s. Artists played secret shows in abandoned buildings. Electronic music was more mainstream by the early 2000s. Soundcloud, Spotify, and YouTube grew. This made electronic music easier to create and find. EDM took off in the 2010s. Artists mixed subgenres. People found new music online and at festivals.

ELECTRONIC TIMELINE

1930s
Clara Rockmore begins to play the theremin

1951
A computer first plays digital sound

1970
German group Kraftwerk releases their first album

1958
Daphne Oram opens a BBC studio for experimenting with music and sound

1964
Robert Moog invents a synth that is later used throughout the music industry

DAPHNE ORAM

ROBERT MOOG

1983

MIDI becomes the standard connection between musical instruments and computers

2010

SoundCloud, a platform for posting and sharing music, reaches one million users

BREAKING

"Gangnam Style" mixed K-pop and EDM. It became so popular that it broke YouTube's view counting system.

1977

Frankie Knuckles starts DJing at the Warehouse club in Chicago

1990s

Artists in Berlin hold underground techno parties called raves

2012

PSY's "Gangnam Style" goes viral, becoming the first video to reach one billion YouTube views

FRANKIE KNUCKLES

PSY

INSTRUMENTS

SYNTH

Robert Moog invented the modern synth in 1964. This machine has a keyboard and electronic parts.

MIDI

MIDI stands for Musical Instrument Digital Interface. Instruments and computers use MIDI to communicate. It has been used since 1983.

DRUM MACHINE

Henry Cowell and Leon Theremin made the first drum machine in 1931. Sly & the Family Stone released *There's a Riot Goin' On* forty years later. The hit album featured a drum machine.

DIGITAL COMPUTER

John Vincent Atanasoff and Clifford E. Berry were inventors. They invented a digital computer around 1940. It became popular with musicians after Dave Smith invented MIDI.

DIGITAL SAMPLER

Peter Zinovieff invented the digital sampler in 1969. Artists can remix and borrow sounds from other music. Best-selling artist Stevie Wonder used sampling on his 1979 album. It was called *Journey Through the Secret Life of Plants*.

AWARDS AND HONORS

DAVID GUETTA

GRAMMY AWARDS

The Grammys honor musical artists. They began in 1959. Awards celebrate dance and electronic albums and recordings.

VGX AWARDS

This award show ran from 2003 to 2013. It celebrated the best computer and video games. These often use electronic music.

2004 VGX AWARDS

BILLBOARD

Billboard magazine has reported on music news since 1894. It publishes charts that rank albums, songs, and artists by popularity. It gives awards to the top artists each year.

MARSHMELLO

ROLLING STONE

Rolling Stone magazine started in 1967. It reports on music, TV, film, politics, and culture. It publishes lists that honor top artists and albums.

TYPES OF ELECTRONIC

SYNTHPOP
(LATER CALLED SYNTHWAVE)

Date Started: 1970s

Traits:
- heavy use of synth
- dreamy sounds
- catchy rhythms

Song:
"Jesu, Joy of Man's Desiring," by Wendy Carlos

AMBIENT

Date Started: 1970s

Traits:
- no clear beginning or end
- lacks conventional rhythms
- sustained tones

Song:
"1/1" by Brian Eno

THE WAREHOUSE

House music gets its name from the Warehouse. It was a Chicago club. This style of music was first played there.

THE KLF

DONNA SUMMER

TRANCE

Date Started: 1990s

Traits:
- uplifting energy
- repetitive beats
- extended sections of sound

Song: "Last Train to Trancentral" by the KLF

HOUSE

Date Started: 1980s

Traits:
- dance beats
- rhythms created with a drum machine
- soulful vocals

Song: "I Feel Love" by Donna Summer

DUBSTEP

Date Started: early 2000s

Traits:

- blends half-time and double-time tempos
- syncopation
- extended bass notes with a wobbling sound

Song: "Scary Monsters and Nice Sprites" by Skrillex

DRUM AND BASS

Date Started: early 1990s

Traits:

- complex drum patterns
- deep bass
- layered samples

Song: "Inner City Life" by Goldie

TRAP

Date Started: early 2000s

Traits:

◊ complex drum patterns
◊ heavy bass
◊ rapid hi-hats

Song: "Soy Peor" by Bad Bunny

HYPERPOP

Date Started: 2010s

Traits:

◊ borrowed sounds
◊ heavily processed vocals
◊ glitchy effects

Song: "BIPP" by SOPHIE

ELECTRONIC PROFILES

WENDY CARLOS

Wendy Carlos is a groundbreaking American musician and composer. She is famous for her synth work.

CREATIVE THINKER

Carlos played piano and composed music as a child. She built a sound system for her family. She won a scholarship for designing a computer.

Birthday:
November 14, 1939

Hometown:
Pawtucket, Rhode Island

Types of Music:
ambient, synthpop, classical

First Hit Song:
"Air on a G String" (1968)

TIMELINE

1949
Carlos writes her first song at age 10

1964
She meets Robert Moog

1970
Carlos wins three Grammy awards for *Switched-On Bach*

MULTITALENTED MUSICIAN

Carlos helped Robert Moog improve his synth models. She reinvented classical music as electronic music. She also created original music on the synth. She was the first transgender person to win a Grammy.

HIT RELEASES

- ***Switched-On Bach*** **(1968)**
- ***The Well-Tempered Synthesizer*** **(1969)**
- ***Wendy Carlos's Clockwork Orange (Complete Original Score)*** **(1972)**
- ***TRON Original Soundtrack*** **(1982)**
- ***Secrets of Synthesis*** **(1987)**

SYNTH SOUNDS PIONEER

Carlos improved synth design. Her compositions brought synth sounds into the mainstream.

1982

Carlos writes the score for the movie *TRON*

1986

***Switched-On Bach* becomes the second classical and first electronic music album to sell one million copies**

BRIAN ENO

Brian Eno is a British keyboardist, singer, composer, and producer. He created the ambient music genre.

ARTISTIC IDEAS

Eno was an art student when he started making electronic music. He used tape recording to create new sounds. He put them on his first album.

PRODUCING HITS

Eno produced many hit albums for other artists. He also composed music for movies, TV shows, and Microsoft Windows.

REBOOT

The Microsoft Windows 95 reboot chime is famous. It is even included in the National Recording Registry.

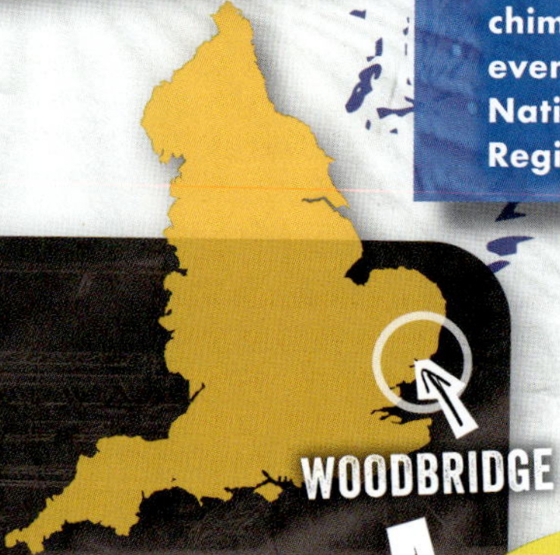

Birthday:
May 15, 1948

Hometown:
Woodbridge, Suffolk, England

Type of Music:
ambient

First Hit Song:
"Baby's On Fire" (1974)

CREATING A GENRE

Eno's style and sounds were once unusual. Now they are a part of our culture.

HIT RELEASES

- *(No Pussyfooting)* (1973)
- *Another Day on Earth* (2005)
- *The Ship* (2016)
- *Music for Installations* (2018)
- *Film Music 1976–2020* (2020)

TIMELINE

1973
Eno releases his first album, *(No Pussyfooting)*

1980
He produces the Talking Heads album *Remain in Light*

1984
He produces U2's album *The Unforgettable Fire*

1995
He composes the Microsoft Windows 95 reboot chime

2020
He releases *Film Music 1967–2020*

TANGERINE DREAM

Tangerine Dream are a legendary German band. Their changing lineup has created new music for decades.

BUILDING FOUNDATIONS

Edgar Froese started and led the band. Their music became the foundations for today's ambient and trance genres.

HIT RELEASES

Atem
(1973)

Phaedra
(1974)

Legend (Original Motion Picture Soundtrack)
(1986)

Canyon Dreams
(1991)

Raum
(2022)

TIMELINE

1973
A BBC Radio DJ nominates *Atem* for Album of the Year

1974
***Phaedra* hits number 15 on UK album charts**

1986
The movie *Legend* comes out in North America

LEGENDARY EXPERIMENTS

Tangerine Dream experimented with synth sounds. They used the violin, guitar, and saxophone. They composed music for movies, including *Legend*. A popular video game features their music.

SHIFTING SOUNDS

The band continued after Froese died in 2015. Their sound was always shifting. Their new music still attracts new listeners.

Notable Members:
Edgar Froese, Christopher Franke, Peter Baumann, Thorsten Quaeschning, Hoshiko Yamane, Paul Frick

Dates Active:
1967–today

Place Formed:
Berlin, Germany

Types of Music:
house, pop, disco, R & B

First Hit Song:
"Ultima Thule, Pt. 1" (1971)

1992
Canyon Dreams is nominated for a Grammy Award

2013
The band wins the VGX Award for best soundtrack in a computer game

THE KLF

The KLF were fearless, controversial, and creative.

BREAKING BOUNDARIES

Bill Drummond and Jimmy Cauty formed the JAMs in 1987. They sampled the Beatles, ABBA, and Led Zeppelin. They got in trouble for breaking copyright laws. They soon changed their name to the KLF.

Notable Members:
Bill Drummond, Jimmy Cauty

Place Formed
London, England

Dates Active:
1989–1992

Types of Music:
ambient, trance

First Hit Songs:
"What Time Is Love?" (1988)

HIT RELEASES

- *1987 (The JAMs 45 Edits)* (1987)
- *Who Killed the JAMs?* (1988)
- *Chill Out* (1990)
- *The White Room* (1991)

STANDING STRONG

The KLF worked with artists from other genres, including country and heavy metal. They demanded world peace. They deleted their music and refused to make more until this could be achieved.

FUTURE FOCUSED

The KLF were unconventional. They showed artists can use music to make real change.

"K CERA CERA"

Israel and Palestine made a peace agreement in 1993. The KLF honored it by releasing the song "K Cera Cera (War Is Over If You Want It)."

TIMELINE

1987
Drummond and Cauty form the JAMs (Justified Ancients of Mu Mu)

1988
Their song "Doctorin' the Tardis" reaches number one on the UK charts

1989
They change their name to the KLF (Kopyright Liberation Front)

1991
They release "Justified & Ancient," featuring country singer Tammy Wynette

1992
They shock the audience at the Brit Awards with a heavy metal version of their popular song "3 a.m. Eternal"

DAFT PUNK

Daft Punk were a groundbreaking French duo.

GENRE SWITCH

Thomas Bangalter and Guy-Manuel de Homem-Christo met as students. They played in a rock band together. They liked EDM and switched genres.

Notable Members:
Thomas Bangalter, Guy-Manuel de Homem-Christo

Dates Active:
1993–2021

Place Formed:
Paris, France

Types of Music:
house, pop, disco, R & B

First Hit Song:
"Da Funk" (1995)

TIMELINE

1997
Daft Punk release their first album, featuring the single "Around the World"

2009
Daft Punk win their first Grammys

2010
TRON: Legacy comes out

FAR-REACHING FAME

With their second album, Daft Punk started appearing as robots. Their song "Around the World" was popular all over the globe. It played in dance clubs. They composed the soundtrack for the movie *TRON: Legacy*.

SIGHTS AND SOUNDS

Daft Punk approached music with a sense of adventure. They pioneered exciting sounds. Their robot personas added visual mystery.

HIT RELEASES

Homework (1997)

Discovery (2001)

Human After All (2005)

Random Access Memories (2013)

2014
Random Access Memories **wins four Grammys including Album of the Year.**

2021
Daft Punk break up

SKRILLEX

Skrillex is a Grammy-winning musician and producer. He is known for mixing genres.

NICKNAME

The name Skrillex comes from an old screen name the artist used.

REINVENTING HIMSELF

Skrillex played guitar in a band as a teenager. He started making music as a DJ in 2008.

Birthday:
January 15, 1988

Hometown:
Los Angeles, California

Types of Music:
dubstep, house, techno

First Hit Song:
"Scary Monsters and Nice Sprites" (2010)

BUILDING BRIDGES

Skrillex is known for blending electronic music with pop, metal, and other styles. His music has made electronic music popular across generations.

HIT MAKER

Skrillex has won nine Grammys. He has composed music for movies, including *Wreck-It Ralph*. He also produces hit songs with other artists. He and Diplo formed Jack Ü in 2013. Their popular song "Where Are Ü Now" featured Justin Bieber.

HIT RELEASES

My Name Is Skrillex
(2010)

Scary Monsters and Nice Sprites
(2010)

Bangarang
(2011)

Quest for Fire
(2023)

Don't Get Too Close
(2023)

TIMELINE

2008
Skrillex starts performing as a DJ

2010
Skrillex releases his EP *My Name Is Skrillex* for free online

2012
He wins Best Dance Recording, Best Dance/Electronica Album, and Best Remixed Nonclassical Recording at the Grammys

2013
He wins three more Grammys and a *Billboard* Music Award

2024
He wins his ninth Grammy Award

PORTER ROBINSON

Porter Robinson is an American singer, songwriter, DJ, and producer.

DEDICATED MUSIC MAKER

Robinson started making music when he was 12. He recorded his first EP on Skrillex's label. Soon he was making remixes for artists Lady Gaga and Avicii.

FIGHTING CANCER

Robinson started the Robinson Malawi Fund in 2019. The charity helps kids with Burkitt lymphoma. Robinson's brother had this type of cancer.

CHAPEL HILL

Birthday:
July 15, 1992

Hometown:
Chapel Hill, North Carolina

Types of Music:
EDM, hyperpop, trance

First Hit Song:
"Language" (2012)

TIMELINE

2011
Robinson's first EP, *Spitfire*, comes out

2012
"Language" debuts at number nine on the UK Top 40 chart

2019
He creates the Robinson Malawi Fund to raise money for Burkitt lymphoma, a form of cancer

GIVING BACK

Robinson released some of his music as Virtual Self. His song "Ghost Voices" was nominated for a Grammy. He started his own music festival, Second Sky. It raises money for kids with cancer.

MAKING MEANING

Robinson has made music about his feelings and struggles. His work offers new ways to tell personal stories.

HIT RELEASES

- ***Spitfire*** **(2011)**
- ***Worlds*** **(2014)**
- ***Nurture*** **(2021)**

2019
He hosts the first Second Sky music festival

2021
His second full album, *Nurture*, comes out

CHARLI XCX

Charli XCX is a British experimental singer and songwriter. She has won three Grammys.

EARLY AMBITION

Charli XCX recorded her first mixtape when she was 14. She shared songs online. She performed at parties.

MAJOR IMPACT

Charli XCX formed her own record label. She produced experimental music. Her album *BRAT* inspired memes, dances, and political leaders. Kamala Harris used parts of the album when she ran for president.

Birthday:
August 2, 1992

Hometown:
Cambridge, England

Types of Music:
hyperpop, synthpop

First Hit Song:
"I Love It" (2012)

PUSHING FORWARD

Charli XCX uses music to create new vibes and name new ideas. Many have become part of our culture.

HIT RELEASES

- ***True Romance*** **(2013)**
- ***Sucker*** **(2014)**
- ***Charli*** **(2019)**
- ***Crash*** **(2022)**
- ***BRAT*** **(2024)**

TIMELINE

2008
Charli XCX shares her music on MySpace

2013
She releases her first album, *True Romance*

2016
She creates her own record label called Vroom Vroom Recordings

2024
She releases *BRAT*

2025
She wins three Grammys for her work on *BRAT*

SOPHIE

SOPHIE was a British experimental music producer.

CAREER BEGINNINGS

As a child, SOPHIE went to live music shows with her father. She learned to make music on a synth.

Birthday:
September 17, 1986

Death:
January 30, 2021

Hometown:
Northampton, England

Types of Music:
hyperpop, ambient, techno

First Hit Song:
"Nothing More to Say/Eeehhh" (2013)

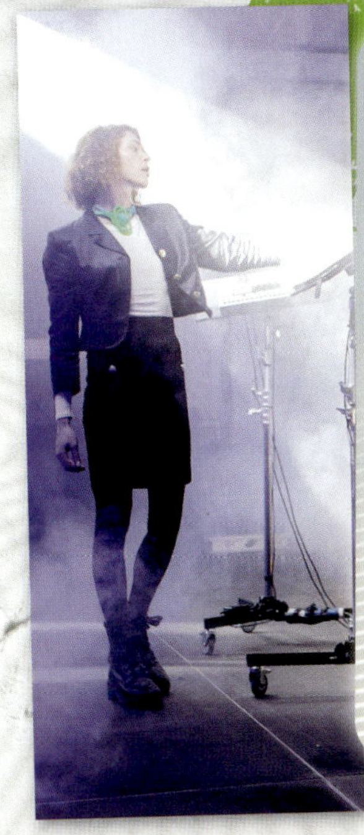

HIT RELEASES

Product (2015)

Oil of Every Pearl's Un-Insides (2018)

SOPHIE (2024)

CAREER HIGHLIGHTS

SOPHIE's album *Oil of Every Pearl's Un-Insides* was nominated for a Grammy. She created music with other influential artists including Charli XCX and Madonna. Her second album was released after she died in an accident.

LEGACY

SOPHIE mixed mainstream and experimental sounds. Her work revolutionized electronic music.

TIMELINE

2008
SOPHIE starts performing in Berlin, Germany, with the group Motherland

2015
SOPHIE releases *Product* and produces a single with Madonna

2016
***Vroom Vroom,* an EP SOPHIE made with Charli XCX, is released**

2018
***Oil of Every Pearl's Un-Insides* is nominated for a Grammy**

2024
The album *SOPHIE* is released

100 GECS

100 gecs is an American duo. It is made up of Laura Les and Dylan Brady.

DIY

Les and Brady released music on their own for years. Then they signed with Atlantic Records.

Notable Members:
Laura Les, Dylan Brady

Dates Active:
2015–present

Place Formed:
St. Louis, Missouri

Type of Music:
hyperpop

First Hit Song:
"Money Machine" (2019)

TIMELINE

2015
Laura Les and Dylan Brady start making music together

2019
Rolling Stone magazine names them an "Artist You Need to Know"

STARTING YOUNG

Rolling Stone named the duo an "Artist You Need to Know." In 2020, 100 gecs headlined an online music festival. The event took place in the video game *Minecraft*.

HIT RELEASES

100 gecs (2016)

1000 gecs (2019)

1000 gecs and The Tree of Clues (2020)

Snake Eyes (2022)

10,000 gecs (2023)

MUSICAL MIX

Their second album includes songs called "Frog on the Floor" and "I Got My Tooth Removed." The music is serious. But it also shows a sense of humor.

2020 They headline the *Minecraft* Square Garden festival

2020 They sign with Atlantic Records

2023 They release their second full-length album

MARSHMELLO

Marshmello is an American EDM producer and DJ. His biggest hit is "Happier." As of 2026, the song had 1.3 billion views on YouTube.

GETTING DISCOVERED

Marshmello first got attention when he posted remixes on SoundCloud. He called himself Dotcom. After a few years, he signed a recording deal.

MASKMELLO

His first album, *Joytime*, was a hit. Marshmello started to get famous. But people did not know his real identity. He performed with a helmet over his face.

Birthday:
May 19, 1992

Hometown:
Philadelphia, Pennsylvania

Types of Music:
EDM, pop, hip-hop, reggaeton, dubstep, trap

First Hit Song:
"Alone" (2016)

LEGACY

Marshmello showed the world that music and celebrity do not have to mix. His music could stand on its own.

HIT RELEASES

- ***Joytime*** (2016)
- ***Joytime II*** (2018)
- ***Marshmello Fortnite Extended Set*** (2019)
- ***Shockwave*** (2021)
- ***The Roots*** (2024)

TIMELINE

2014
Marshmello signs with Buygore Records as Dotcom

2015
He starts using the name Marshmello

2017
He collaborates with Selena Gomez on the song "Wolves"

2019
Fortnite Battle Royale hosts a Marshmello concert online

2022
He is nominated for a Grammy

JANE REMOVER

Jane Remover is an American singer, songwriter, and producer.

SHARING THEIR SOUND

Jane Remover shared their song "what's my age again?" on SoundCloud. Then the song spread on Twitter.

SHARING THEIR SOUND

Their song "homeswitcher" had 100,000 streams in its first two weeks. Fans loved Jane Remover for expressing honest emotions and energy. The artist came out as transgender in 2022. They changed their name to Jane Remover. They removed four songs from the EP *Teen Week* to honor the change.

TIMELINE

2020
"what's my age again?" is released on SoundCloud

2021
***Teen Week* is released**

2021
"homeswitcher" has 100,000 streams on SoundCloud in two weeks

SOUND FOUNDER

Jane Remover has shown how an artist controls their own music and career. They also created a new genre called dariacore. It was inspired by the TV series *Daria*.

DARIA

Daria **was an animated series that ran from 1997 to 2002. The main character was a smart, cynical teenager. Her name was Daria Morgendorffer.**

HIT RELEASES

- ***Teen Week*** **(2021)**
- ***Dariacore*** **(2021)**
- ***Frailty*** **(2021)**
- ***Census Designated*** **(2023)**
- ***Revengeseekerz*** **(2025)**

Birthday:
September 26, 2003

Hometown:
Newark, New Jersey

Types of Music:
electronic pop, hip-hop, rock, digicore

First Hit Song:
"homeswitcher" (2021)

2022
The artist changes their name to Jane Remover

2025
Jane Remover headlines their first concert tour

THE FUTURE OF ELECTRONIC

Electronic music is all about experimentation. It started with inventions such as the tape recorder, synth, and computer. New technology pushes electronic music artists to try new things.

HONEY DIJON

Modern musical artists work differently because of what is available to them. Holly Herndon collaborates with AI. Deadmau5 works in virtual reality. Artists continue to mix elements from different genres. Honey Dijon and Tiësto headline festivals around the world. As more technology is invented, music will continue evolving. It will change the ways artists produce music. In electronic music, there is always more to explore.

GLOSSARY

AI—a computer's ability to do something a human mind can do; AI is short for artificial intelligence.

collaborates—works with someone else on a project

composers—people who write or create music

compositions—written pieces of music

copyright—related to the exclusive legal right given to artists to use their own material and allow others to use it

culture—the beliefs, arts, and ways of life in a place or society

duo—a group of two

generations—groups of people who were born around the same time

genres—categories for types of music

glitchy effects—deliberate use of sounds from imperfections

headlined—played as the lead performer at a concert or event

inspired—gave someone an idea about what to do or create

LGBTQ+—a community of people who identify as something other than heterosexual or the gender they were assigned at birth; LGBTQ+ stands for Lesbian, Gay, Bisexual, Transgender, Queer and other identities.

mainstream—common and shared by a large audience

melodies—series of lyrics and sounds that are arranged with a rhythm

mixtape—a collection of songs, usually released for free by artists online

nominates—chooses as a candidate for an award

personas—roles or characters

processed—manipulated with digital tools

rhythms—repeated patterns of movement or sound

scholarship—money to support a student's education

spliced—cut and combined in new ways

subgenres—smaller, more specific types of music within a genre

sustained—continuing for a long period without interruption

syncopation—changing the rhythm of music to emphasize different beats

synthesizers—electronic musical instruments that can create sounds and change existing sounds

tape recorder—a device that records sounds on magnetic tape and plays them back

theremin—an electronic instrument played by moving hands around the instrument without touching it

tones—musical sounds related to pitch, quality, and strength

vocoders—devices that alter a recording of someone's voice to make new sounds

WRITE ABOUT IT!

- **Which artist** do you think has had the biggest impact on electronic music?
- What are some of your favorite electronic music subgenres? **Why do you like them?**
- How do you think electronic music will continue to **change** in the future?

ALSO CHECK OUT

INDEX

The images in this book are reproduced through the courtesy of: Sevastsyanau Uladzimir, front cover (hero); Dmytro Vietrov, front cover (keyboardist); undefined undefined, front cover (audio mixer); Christian Bertrand, front cover (female singer), p. 34 (middle right); Tuomas Vitikainen/ Wikimedia Commons, pp. 3 (Charli XCX), 35 (Charli XCX, middle); John Shearer/ Getty Images, pp. 3 (Marshmello), 40 (Marshmello, left); Kathy Hutchin pp. 3 (Skrillex), 15 (top left), 30 (Skrillex, middle), 31 (top), 41 (bottom); Michael Mastre/ Alamy Stock Photo, p. 4 (top); Frédéric Vicomte/ Wikimedia Commons, p. 4 (bottom); Lionel FLUSIN/ Getty Images, p. 5 (left); HENRY NICHOLLS/ Getty Images, p. 5 (right); Renato Toppo/ Wikimedia Commons, pp. 6, 10 (1930s); Daily Herald Archive/ Getty Images, pp. 7 (top), 10 (1958); Mirrorpix/ Getty Images, p. 7 (bottom); ZUMA Press/ Alamy Stoc Photo, pp. 8 (top), 9 (top right), 31 (middle); Gorodenkoff, p. 8 (left); Claire Greenway/ Getty Images, p. 8 (bottom); Jean-Marc Lallemand/ Alamy Stock Photo, p. 9 (top left); Fraser Gray/ Alam Stock Photo, p. 9 (bottom); Rubens Ben/ Wikimedia Commons, p. 9 (inset); Bettmann/ Getty Images, pp. 10 (1955), 13 (top, bottom); Michael Tullberg/ Getty Images, p. 11 (1977); DC Studio, p. 11 (1983); Mehaniq, p. 11 (2010); Debby Wong, pp. 11 (2012, Gangnam Style), 34 (bottom); Ben Houdijk, pp. 1 (top), 23 (top right); PrinceOfLove, p. 12 (MIDI); Cindy Ord/ Get Images, p. 12 (bottom); New York Public Library; Music Division/ Wikimedia Commons, p. 12 (Henry Cowell); s_bukley, p. 14 (top left); Bernd Schwabe/ Wikimedia Commons, pp. 14 (top right), 20 (grammy), 28 (grammy), 29 (grammy), 31 (grammy), 35 (grammy), 37 (grammy), 41 (grammy); Jeff Kravitz, Getty Images, p.p 14 (bottom left), 28 (top); Jesse Grant/ Getty Images, p. 14 (bottom right); Gustavo Caballero/ Getty Images, p. 15 (top right); dennizn, p. 15 (bottom); Pictorial Press/ Alamy Stock Photos, p. 16 (top); Leonard M. DeLessio/ Getty Images, pp. 16 (bottom), 20 (top, bottom left, bottom middle), 21; kpa/ Arthur Grimm/ Getty Images, p. 17 (left); JMEnternational/ Getty Images, pp. 17 (right), 26 (top right); MusicLive/ Alamy Stock Photo, p. 18 (bottom left); Carlos Osorio/ Getty Images, pp. 18-19; Sipa USA/ Alamy Stock Photo, p. 19 (top); Joseph Okpako/ Getty Images, pp. 19 (bottom), 30 (top left), 37 (middle Wangkun Jia, p. 20 (Pawtucket); Moog Music/ Norlin/ Wikimed Commons, p. 20 (1964); Brian Cooke/ Getty Images, p. 22 (top, bottom); Garry Knight/ Wikimedia Commons, p. 22 (middle left); CapturePB, p. 22 (middle right); Ronnie, p. 22 (Woodbridge); Richard Creamer/ Getty Images, p. 23 (middle); Michael Putland Getty Images, pp. 24 (left), 25 (top); Ralf Roletschek/ Wikimedia Commons, p. 24 (right); Virginia Turbett/ Getty Images, p. 25 (bottom); JFL Photography, p. 25 (Berlin); Martyn Goodacre/ Getty Images, p. 26 (left); Roberta Parkin/ Getty Images, p. 26 (bottom); Sven Hansche, p. 26 (London); Tabatha Fireman/ Getty Images, p. 27 (top); Richard Martin-Roberts/ Getty Images, p. 27 (bottom); David Axelbank/ Alamy Stock Photo, p. 28 (bottom); saiko3p, p. 28 (Paris); Travis Rigel Lukas Hornung/ Wikimedia Commons, p. 29 (left); Gregg DeGuire/ Getty Images, p. 29 (right); Jgphotographydetroit, p. 30 (middle); Newport Coast Media, p. 30 (Los Angeles); Chelsea Lauren/ Getty Images, p. 3 (bottom); Daniel DeSlover/ Alamy Stock Photo, p. 32 (top left); Frazer Harrison/ Getty Images, pp. 32 (top right), 33 (middle), 36 (top left), 37 (bottom); Dia Dipasupil/ Getty Images, p. 32 (bottom); Grindstone Media Group, p. 32 (Chapel Hill); Weekly Dig/ Wikimedia Commons, p. 33 (left); Jason Koerner/ Getty Images, p. 33 (bottom); Sterling Munksgard, pp. 34 (top), 41 (middle); Anna Hanks/ Wikimedia Commons, p. 34 (middle left); Alexey Fedorenko, p. 34 (Cambridge); DFree, p. 35 (right); Daniele Baldi/ Alamy Stock Photo, pp. 36 (middle), 37 (top); Alt Shah, p. 36 (Northhampton); Matt Winkelmeyer/ Getty Images, p, 36 (bottom); Geoffrey Clowes, p. 38 (top, middle); Mat Hayward/ Getty Images, pp. 38, 39 (top); Brennen Higgins, p. 38 (St. Louis); Astrida Valigorsky/ Getty Images, p. 39 (middle Tinseltown, p. 40 (bottom); Michael Bogner, p. 40 (Philadelphia); Arturo Holmes/ Getty Images, p. 41 (top); Angel/ Wikimedia Commons, p. 42 (top left); Rick Kern/ Getty Images, pp. 42 (righ bottom), 43 (top, bottom); Christopher Boswell, p. 43 (Newark); KinoMasterskaya, p. 44 (top); Dave Benett/ Getty Images, p. 44 (bottom left); SeventyFour, p. 44 (bottom right); Scott Roth/ AP Images, p. 45 (top); Felipe Trueba/ Getty Images, p. 45 (middle) Santiago Felipe/ Getty Images, p. 45 (bottom).